THE ULTIMATE JOKE BOOK FOR 10 YEAR OLD KIDS!

CONTAINS 500 RIB-TICKLERS!

COMPILED BY MICHELLE JAY

First published in Great Britain in 2023 by Frosty Hollow Publishing.

Copyright (c) 2023

ISBN: 9798396819818

All rights reserved No part of this publication may be reproduced, stored in a retrieval system, or transmitted by any means, without the prior permission in writing of the publisher, nor be otherwise circulated in any form of binding or cover other than that in which it is published and without a similar condition including this condition being imposed on the subsequent purchaser.

CONTENTS

Chapter 1: Silly Side Splitters   5
Chapter 2: School Shenanigans   23
Chapter 3: Gross Gags   37
Chapter 4: Screwball Sports   46
Chapter 5: Slapstick Superheroes   56
Chapter 6: Animal Antics   61
Chapter 7: Seaside Silliness   80
Chapter 8: Dizzy Dinosaurs   89
Chapter 9: Daft Doctors   97
Chapter 10: Cosmic Comedy   102
Chapter 11: Door Knockers   110
Chapter 12: Spooky Sniggers   118
Chapter 13: Funny Food   133
Chapter 14: Waiter Wisecracks   143
Chapter 15: Christmas Crackers   147

INTRODUCTION

To all the laughter seekers, mischief makers, and smile enthusiasts, this book is for you! May its pages ignite endless fits of giggles, bring joy to your hearts, and remind you of the power of humour.

From the cheesy puns to the clever one-liners, may these jokes brighten your days and lighten your spirits.

Laughter is the best medicine, and it is my sincerest hope that this collection brings you heaps of it!

This book is dedicated to the three little jokesters in my life, Georgie, Ali and Izzy, who keep me laughing each and every day. This book is dedicated to you!

CHAPTER 1: SILLY SIDESPLITTERS!

STEP INTO THE UPROARIOUS REALM OF "SILLY SIDESPLITTERS" WHERE A WORLD OF LAUGHTER AWAITS!

BRACE YOURSELF FOR AN UNFORGETTABLE JOURNEY THROUGH A WHIMSICAL WONDERLAND OF WORDPLAY AND ZANY SCENARIOS THAT WILL HAVE YOU CLUTCHING YOUR SIDES IN FITS OF GIGGLES.

SO BUCKLE UP, FASTEN YOUR SEAT-BELT, AND GET READY TO EMBARK ON AN EPIC QUEST FOR LAUGHTER, WHERE EVERY TURN OF THE PAGE HOLDS A SURPRISE THAT WILL LEAVE YOU HOWLING WITH DELIGHT!

Why can't Elsa from Frozen have a balloon?
Because she will "let it go, let it go!"

How did the mobile phone propose to his girlfriend?
He gave her a ring!

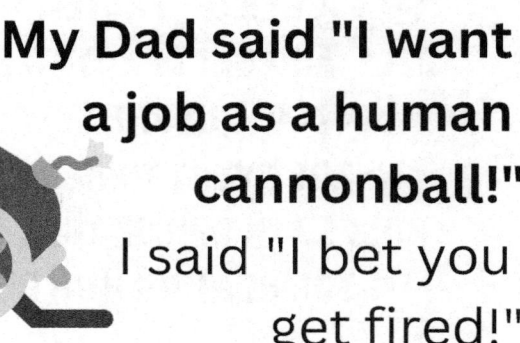

My Dad said "I want a job as a human cannonball!"
I said "I bet you get fired!"

Why shouldn't you trust stairs?

Because they are always up to something!

What kind of tree fits in the palm of your hand?

A palm tree!

What is a tornado's favorite game?

Twister!

Why did the mobile phone get glasses?

Because she lost all her contacts!

Where do dolls like to eat?
At a Barbie-cue!

What did the left eye say to the right eye?
Between us, something smells!

Why did the teddy bear say no to dessert?
Because it was already stuffed!

What do you call a belt made out of watches?
A waist of time!

What does the King do when he belches?
Issues a royal pardon!

Why was the broom late?
Because he over-swept!

Why did the bike fall over?
It was two-tyred!

What happened to the burglar who fell in the concrete mixer?
He became a hardened criminal!

Why are eye shadow and lipstick never mad at each other?
Because they always make-up!

What did the lift say when he sneezed?
I'm coming down with something!

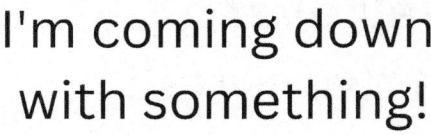

How do you make a hot dog stand?
Steal its chair!

What is a computer's favorite snack?
Computer chips!

What's a frog's favourite drink?
Croaka Cola!

What do you call someone with no body or nose?
Nobody knows!

Why did the man put his money in the freezer?
He wanted cold hard cash!

What's the difference between a snowman and a snow-woman?
Snow balls!

What did the stamp say to the envelope?
"Stick with me and we'll go places!"

What is brown, hairy and wears sunglasses?
A coconut on holiday!

What's a pirate's favourite letter?
Arrrrrr!

What's rain's favourite accessory?
A rainbow!

What vitamin helps you to see?
Vitamin C!

Who wrote the book *How to Make A Million*?
Robin Banks!

What did the judge say when the skunk walked into the courtroom?
"Odour in the court!"

Did you hear about the person who invented knock knock jokes?
She won the no bell prize!

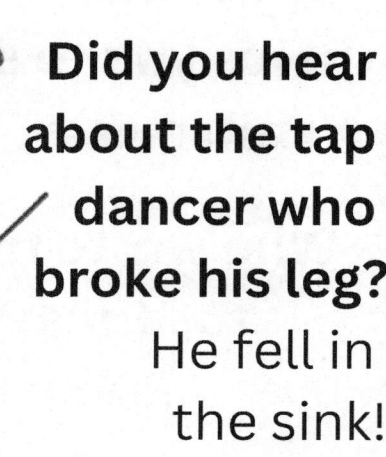

Did you hear about the tap dancer who broke his leg?
He fell in the sink!

Why did the genie get angry?
Because he was rubbed the wrong way!

What's brown and sticky?
A stick! Duh!

Why can't the strawberry cross the road?
He'll cause a traffic jam!

What contests do skunks win at school?
The smelling bee!

What did one hat say to the other?
"You stay here, I'll go on ahead!"

Why did the doctor carry a red pen?
In case he needed to draw blood!

What does a cloud wear under his raincoat?
Thunderwear!

What do you call a fairy who hasn't taken a bath?
Stinker-belle!

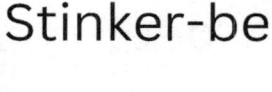

What do you call a boomerang that doesn't come back?
A stick!

What did one wall say to the other wall?
"I'll meet you at the corner!"

What do you call two thieves?
A pair of knickers!

What do you call a snowman in July?
A puddle!

Two pickles fell out of a jar onto the floor. What did one say to the other?
Dill with it!

Why did the bubblegum cross the road?
It was stuck to the chicken's foot!

What do you call a snowman with a six- pack?
The abdominal snowman!

What time is it when the clock strikes 13?

Time to get a new clock!

Why did the coffee file a police report?

Because it got mugged!

Why did the computer go to the doctor?

Because it had a virus!

What did one DNA strand say to the other?

"How do these genes look on me?"

How do you get a squirrel to like you?
Act like a nut!

What did the traffic light say to the car?
"Don't look at me, I'm changing!"

What kind of lion doesn't roar?
A dandelion!

Why don't scientists trust atoms?
Because they make up everything!

What do you call a can opener that doesn't work?
A can't opener!

What kind of car does Mickey Mouse's wife drive?
A Minnie Van!

What do you call an ant who fights crime?
A vigilante!

Which is faster? Hot or cold?
Hot. You can easily catch a cold!

What did one volcano say to the other volcano?
"I lava you!"

Why was the computer cold?
Because it left it's Windows open!

Why was 6 afraid of 7?
Because 7, 8, 9!

What is a tree's favorite drink?
Root beer!

CHAPTER 2: SCHOOL SHENANIGANS!

WELCOME TO "SCHOOL SHENANIGANS" WHERE THE BELL RINGS FOR LAUGHTER AND THE PUNCHLINES ARE AS SHARP AS PENCILS!

GET READY TO TAKE A HILARIOUS DETOUR FROM TEXTBOOKS AND HOMEWORK AS WE DIVE INTO A WORLD OF CLASSROOM COMEDY AND CANTEEN CAPERS.

THESE JOKES WILL HAVE YOU AND YOUR FRIENDS CHUCKLING IN THE CORRIDORS, AS WE EXPLORE THE LIGHTER SIDE OF SCHOOL LIFE WITH PUNNY PUNCHLINES, WITTY TEACHER QUIPS, AND RELATABLE ANTICS THAT WILL MAKE EVEN THE STRICTEST HEAD TEACHER CRACK A SMILE.

SO GRAB YOUR SCHOOL BAG AND GET READY TO LAUGH YOUR WAY THROUGH THIS RIB-TICKLING CHAPTER THAT'S SURE TO EARN YOU AN A+ IN AMUSEMENT!

Why was the maths book sad?
Because it had too many problems!

Why did the student eat his homework?
Because his teacher said it was a piece of cake!

Why did the teacher wear sunglasses to school?
Because her students were so bright!

What kind of teacher passes gas?
A tutor!

Why was the teacher cross-eyed?
Because she couldn't control her pupils!

What animal cheats in exams?
A CHEATah!

Which school supply is king of the classroom?
A ruler!

Why did the boy bring a ladder to school?
Because he wanted to go to high school!

What did you learn in school today?
Not enough! I have to go back tomorrow!

Why did the egg get thrown out of class?
Because he kept telling yolks!

What are the ten things teachers can always count on?
Their fingers!

Why did the triangle go the gym?
To get in shape!

What's a maths teacher's favorite dessert?
Pie!

What school does an ice cream man go to?
Sundae school!

How do bees get to school?
On the school buzzzz!

How did the music teacher get locked in the classroom?
His keys were in the piano!

Why did the school gym close down?
Because it just didn't work out!

Why did the music teacher need a ladder?
To reach the high notes!

What is a witch's favourite subject in school?
Spelling!

Which letter of the alphabet has the most water?
The 'c'!

Why do fireflies get bad grades at school?
Because they're not bright enough!

Why did the teacher go to the beach?
To test the water!

Why do calculators make great friends?
You can always count on them!

Why is 2 + 2 = 5 like your left foot?
It's not right!

What's the worst thing you're likely to find in the school canteen?
The food!

What's better than gym class?
Skipping lessons!

Why did the cyclops close his school?
He only had one pupil!

What is a snake's favourite subject in school?
Hisssstory!

Why did the dog do so well in school?
Because he was the teacher's pet!

Why are fish so smart?
Because they live in schools!

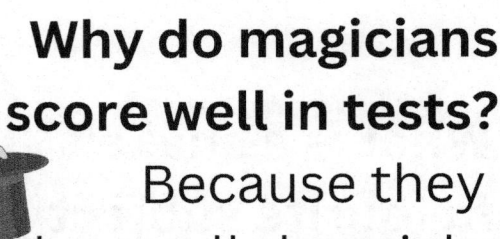

Why do magicians score well in tests?
Because they know all the tricky questions!

Where did the music teacher leave his keys?
In the piano!

What kind of school do surfers go to?
Boarding school!

Why did the jellybean go to school?
He wanted to become a smartie!

What contests do skunks win at school?
The smelling bee!

"Teacher, you wouldn't get mad at me for something I didn't do?"

"No of course not."

"Good because I didn't do my homework!"

What did the teacher say about the pizza student?
There's mushroom for improvement!

Why can't pirates learn the alphabet?
Because they keep getting lost at C!

How do you get straight As?
By using a ruler!

Who is everyone's best friend at school?
The PrinciPAL!

What's a maths teacher's favourite winter sport?
Figure skating!

What did one pencil say to the other on the first day of school?
"Looking sharp!"

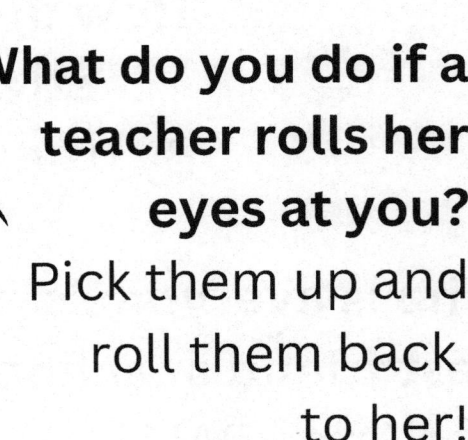

What do you do if a teacher rolls her eyes at you?
Pick them up and roll them back to her!

CHAPTER 3: GROSS GAGS!

HOLD YOUR NOSES AND BRACE YOURSELVES FOR "GROSS GAGS" WHERE HILARITY MEETS THE ICKY AND THE SILLY GETS A BIT SQUISHY!

GET READY TO EMBARK ON A WILD AND WACKY ADVENTURE INTO THE WORLD OF ALL THINGS SLIMY, STINKY, AND DOWNRIGHT DISGUSTING.

FROM BOOGER BATTLES TO FART SYMPHONIES, THESE JOKES WILL HAVE YOU GIGGLING AND GAGGING AT THE SAME TIME.

SO, IF YOU'RE NOT AFRAID TO GET A LITTLE MESSY AND HAVE A STOMACH OF STEEL, DIVE RIGHT INTO THIS CHAPTER THAT'S GUARANTEED TO MAKE YOU LAUGH, CRINGE, AND MAYBE EVEN LOSE YOUR LUNCH (IN A GOOD WAY)!

What did one bogey say to another?
"You think you're funny but you're snot!"

What's the difference between bogies and broccoli?
Kids don't eat broccoli!

What did the nose say to the finger?
"Stop picking on me!"

Why was the nose sad?
Because it didn't get picked!

What monster can sit on the end of your finger?
A bogeyman!

What comes out of your nose at 150 miles per hour?
A Lambogreeny!

How do you make a tissue dance?
You put a boogie in it!

What does a bogey in love tell his girlfriend?
I'm stuck on you!

Why are ninja farts so dangerous?
They're silent but deadly!

Did you hear about the slow student with terrible gas?
He was getting farter and farter behind so his parents hired a tooter!

Why should you never fart on an elevator?
Because it's wrong on so many levels!

I farted at work the other day...and my coworker tried opening the window. It must have been a really bad one - we work on a submarine!

Did you hear about the blind skunk? He feel in love with a fart!

What's the smelliest game in the world? Top Trumps!

What did one toilet say to another?
You look flushed!

Why was Tigger down the toilet?
Because he was looking for Pooh!

What do you call a dog that you find in your toilet?
A poodle!

Why does the toilet paper roll down the hill?
To get to the bottom!

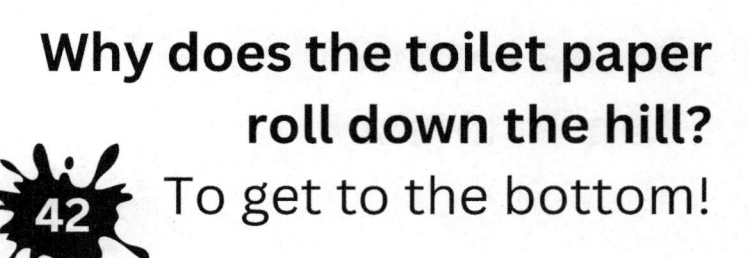

Why does Spider-Man make sure to always flush the toilet?
Because it's his doody!

Poop jokes aren't my favorite jokes?
But they're a solid number two!

If cows could fly, what might you get?
A pat on the head!

What happened to the fly on the toilet seat?
It got peed-off!

Why was the sand wet?
Because the sea weed!

What goes ha ha bonk?
A boy laughing his head off!

What's big, blue and smells horrible?
A monster's bottom!

What leaps out from behind a snowdrift and shows you his butt?
The A-bum-inable snowman!

What's worse than finding a slug in your salad?
Finding half a slug!

CHAPTER 4: SCREWBALL SPORTS!

GET YOUR GAME FACE ON AND JOIN US IN THE UPROARIOUS WORLD OF "SCREWBALL SPORTS"!

FROM TOUCHDOWN TOMFOOLERY TO BASKETBALL BLOOPERS, THIS CHAPTER IS A GRAND SLAM OF LAUGHTER FOR SPORTS ENTHUSIASTS AND JOKESTERS ALIKE. WHETHER YOU'RE A FOOTBALL SUPERSTAR OR A BUDDING GYMNAST, THESE JOKES WILL HAVE YOU ROLLING WITH LAUGHTER ON THE SIDELINES.

SO GRAB YOUR FAVOURITE SPORTS GEAR, WARM UP THOSE FUNNY BONES, AND GET READY TO SCORE BIG WITH THESE RIB-TICKLING JOKES THAT WILL KEEP YOU ENTERTAINED FROM THE FIRST WHISTLE TO THE FINAL BUZZER!

Why don't centipedes play football?
Because by the time they've got their boots on it's time to go home!

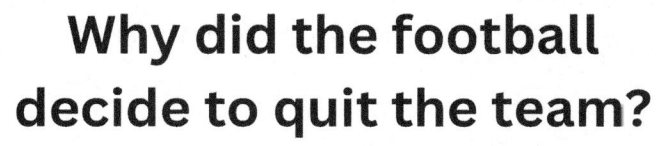

Why did the football decide to quit the team?
He became tired of getting kicked around!

What is a ghost's favorite football position?
Ghoul keeper!

Why shouldn't you play football in the jungle?
There are too many cheetahs!

What lights up a football stadium?
A football match!

When is a baby good at football?
When it's dribbling!

Why did the football player go to jail?
Because he shot the ball!

What time is it when an elephant steps on your football?
Time to get a new ball!

How do you stop squirrels from playing football in the garden?
Hide the ball!
It drives them nuts!

Why can't you play football with pigs?
They hog the ball!

What do football players and magicians have in common?
Both do hat tricks!

What do you call a cat that plays football?
Puss In Boots!

Why shouldn't you ask a footballer to help you with a jigsaw?
Because they keep skipping corners!

Why do basketball courts always get wet?
Because the players always dribble!

What kind of stories do basketball players tell?
Tall tales!

Where do old bowling balls end up?
The gutter!

Why did the American football team go to the bank?
To get their quarterback!

Why can't Cinderella play American football?
Because she's always running away from the ball!

What part of a swimming pool is never the same?
The changing rooms!

What animal is best at hitting a cricket ball?
A bat!

Why is tennis such a loud sport?
The players cause a racket!

Which sport do waiters love?
Tennis because they can serve so well!

Who's the best golfer in the jungle?
Tiger Woods!

Why did the golfer wear two pairs of trousers?
In case he got a hole in one!

How do athletes stay cool?
They stand near the fans!

What do runners do when they forget something?
They jog their memories!

What did the two strings do in the race?
They tied!

What animal is always at a baseball game?
A bat!

Why did it get hot in the baseball stadium after the game?
All of the fans left!

Which sport is always in trouble?
Bad-minton!

CHAPTER 5: SLAPSTICK SUPERHEROES!

GET READY TO UNLEASH YOUR INNER SUPERHERO WITH THE "SLAPSTICK SUPERHEROES" WHERE LAUGHTER MEETS SUPERPOWERS!

JOIN US IN A WORLD OF EXTRAORDINARY HUMOUR AS WE DIVE INTO A COLLECTION OF JOKES THAT WILL HAVE YOU LAUGHING FASTER THAN A SPEEDING BULLET.

FROM WITTY QUIPS BY YOUR FAVORITE CAPED CRUSADERS TO HILARIOUS SUPERHERO MISHAPS, THIS CHAPTER IS PACKED WITH PUNCHLINES THAT ARE MORE POWERFUL THAN A LOCOMOTIVE.

SO PUT ON YOUR CAPE, TIGHTEN YOUR UTILITY BELT, AND PREPARE TO SAVE THE DAY WITH LAUGHTER IN THIS ACTION-PACKED CHAPTER THAT'S SURE TO MAKE YOU FEEL LIKE A COMEDIC SUPERHERO!

How do superheroes prepare their dinner?
They save the food first!

Did you hear the joke about the superhero Wind Man?
I don't know what it was, but apparently, everyone was blown away!

What do you get when you cross a superhero and the Dead Sea?
A Deadpool!

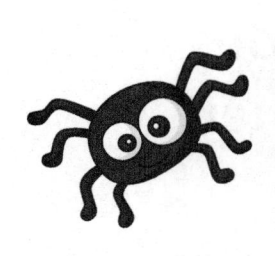

How do the Avengers still see Spider Man when he's out of town?
On his WEB-cam!

What did Iron Man say to Ant Man?
Stop bugging me!

What is a villain's favourite part of the joke?
The punch line!

What do you call a superhero who likes to cook?
Souper-man!

Where does Spider Man hang out in his spare time?
On the World Wide Web!

What do you get when you cross The Incredible Hulk and a flashlight?
A Green Lantern!

What do heroes like Spider Man and Ant Man have in common?
They bug the villains!

Which is Thor's favourite day of the week?
Thors-day, of course!

What do you call a computer superhero?
A screen saver!

How does Darth Vader like his toast?
On the dark side!

What does Spider Man do for a living?
He's a web designer!

CHAPTER 6: ANIMAL ANTICS!

WELCOME TO THE WILD AND WHIMSICAL WORLD OF "ANIMAL ANTICS",

WHERE LAUGHTER ROARS AND GIGGLES SWING FROM BRANCH TO BRANCH! PREPARE FOR A ZOO-TASTIC ADVENTURE AS WE UNLEASH A MENAGERIE OF HILARIOUS ANIMAL PUNS AND RIB-TICKLING RIDDLES.

FROM CHEEKY MONKEYS TO PUNNY PENGUINS, THIS CHAPTER IS PACKED WITH LAUGHS THAT WILL MAKE EVEN THE GRUMPIEST GRIZZLY BEAR CRACK A SMILE.

SO GATHER ROUND, ANIMAL LOVERS, AND GET READY TO EMBARK ON A HILARIOUS SAFARI OF HUMOUR THAT WILL HAVE YOU ROARING WITH LAUGHTER UNTIL THE COWS COME HOME!

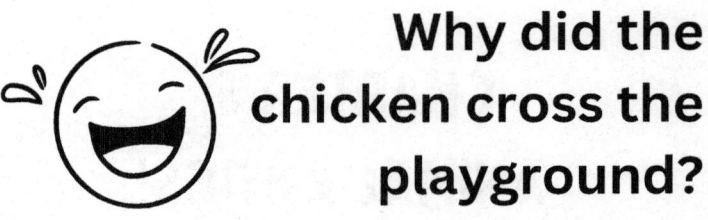

Why did the chicken cross the playground?
To get to the other slide!

What event do spiders love to attend?
Webbings!

What kind of photos will you find on a turtle's phone?
SHELLfies!

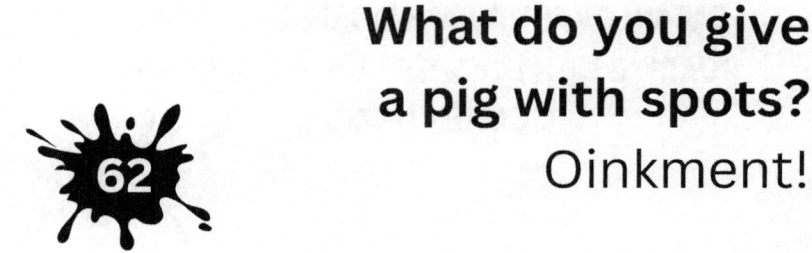

What do you give a pig with spots?
Oinkment!

What did the llama say when he got kicked out of the zoo?
"Alpaca my bags!"

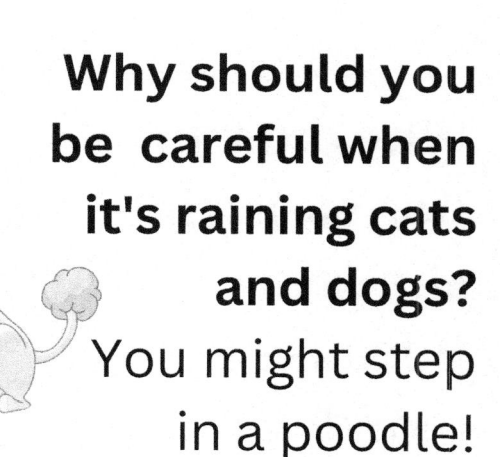

Why should you be careful when it's raining cats and dogs?
You might step in a poodle!

What did the leopard say when he ate the explorer?
"Mmmm, that hit the spot!"

What's black and white, black and white, black and white?
A penguin rolling down a hill!

Why did the dog sit in the shade?
Because it didn't want to be a hot dog!

What do you get if you cross a skunk and a pair of rubber boots?
Smelly wellies!

What do you get if you cross a crocodile with a camera?
A snapshot!

What do you call a pile of cats?
A meowtain!

Why do giraffes have long necks?
Because they have smelly feet!

Why do hummingbirds hum?
Because they don't know the words!

What do you get if you cross a parrot with a centipede?
A walkie talkie!

Why aren't dogs very good dancers?
Because they've got two left feet!

What do you call a rabbit with nits?
Bugs Bunny!

What do you call a hippo with a messy room?
A hippopota-mess!

What do you give a seasick elephant?
An awful lot of room!

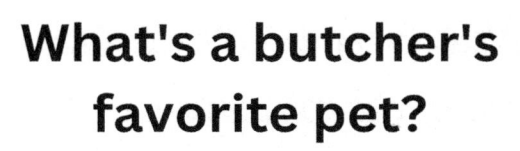

What's a butcher's favorite pet?
A sausage dog!

What do you call a cow that cuts grass?
A lawn moooooooer!

What did Tom get when he locked Jerry in the freezer?
Mice cubes!

Why do cows wear bells?
Because their horns don't work!

What do you call a cow in an earthquake?
A milkshake!

What do you call a baby whale that cries a lot?
A little blubber!

How do you stop a skunk from smelling?
Hold his nose!

**What do you get when
you cross a cow
with a duck?**
Milk and quackers!

**Why do ducks have
tail feathers?**
To hide it's butt
quack!

**Why were the elephants
arrested when
they went swimming?**
They couldn't keep their
trunks up!

What do you call a bear with no teeth?
A gummy bear!

Why do bees have sticky hair?
Because they use honeycombs!

What do you call a lazy kangaroo?
A pouch potato!

What does an owl do when you tell it a joke?
Hoots with laughter!

What do you call a sheep with no legs?
A cloud!

Why did the fox cough?
He had a hare stuck in his throat!

What do you call a sleeping bull?
A bulldozer!

Why do elephants never use computers?
They're afraid of mice!

Why do seagulls fly over the sea?
Because if they flew over the bay, they would be bagels!

What do you get when you cross a sheep with a kangaroo?
A woolly jumper!

Why wouldn't the piglets listen to their dad?
They thought he was such an old boar!

Why did the chicken join the band?
Because it had drumsticks!

What do you call a pig that does karate?
A pork chop!

What do you call a cow that plays a musical instrument?
A moosician!

What do you call a bear with no ears?
B!

What do cats eat for breakfast?
Mice Krispies!

Where do tadpoles change?
In a croakroom!

What did the duck say when it bought lipstick?
"Put it on my bill!"

What do you get when you cross a snake with a pie?
A python!

What would you do if an elephant sat in front of you at a movie ?
Miss most of the movie!

What do you get if you cross a skunk with a boomerang?
A smell you can't get rid of!

What happened to the leopard, after he had a bath every day of the week?
He was spotless!

What did the buffalo say when his son left?
"Bison!"

What do you call a pig with eyes?
Piiig!

What kind of dog can tell the time?
A watch dog!

What snakes are good at doing maths?
Adders!

What do you call a duck that gets all As?
A wise quacker!

Why couldn't the pony sing a lullaby?
She was a little horse!

Why do porcupines always win the game?
They have the most points!

Where do cows go for entertainment?
The mooooovies!

Why are teddy bears never hungry?
They are always stuffed!

What kind of animal is a slug?
A homeless snail!

What is red and black, red and black, red and black?
A zebra with sunburn!

What do you call a crate full of ducks?
A box of quackers!

What did one firefly say to the other?
"You glow, girl!"

How do you put an elephant in the fridge?
Open the door and put the elephant in!

How do you put a giraffe in the fridge?
Take the elephant out and put the giraffe in!

All but one animal went to the lion's birthday party, who didn't go?
The giraffe! He was in the fridge!

How did the humans get across the alligator infested river?
They just swam across because the alligators were at the lion's birthday party!!

CHAPTER 7: SEASIDE SILLINESS!

GET READY TO MAKE A SPLASH WITH OUR "SEASIDE SILLINESS" CHAPTER, WHERE LAUGHTER AND MARINE MERRIMENT COME TOGETHER IN PERFECT HARMONY!

DIVE INTO A WORLD OF AQUATIC HILARITY AS WE EXPLORE THE DEPTHS OF OCEANIC HUMOUR.

FROM WHALE-SIZED PUNS TO FISHY ONE-LINERS, THESE JOKES ARE SURE TO HAVE YOU GIGGLING LIKE A SCHOOL OF PLAYFUL FUNNY FISH.

SO GRAB YOUR SNORKEL, SAIL AWAY WITH LAUGHTER, AND GET READY TO HAVE A WHALE OF A TIME IN THIS LAUGHTER-FILLED CHAPTER THAT WILL MAKE YOU THE STAR OF THE SEA!

Why did the lobster blush?
Because the sea weed!

Why are fish so clever?
Because they're always in schools!

Who keeps the ocean clean?
The mermaid!

Where do fish sleep?
In a riverbed!

What did the fish say when he swam into a wall?
"Dam!"

What part of the fish weighs the most?
The scales!

How do squid get to school?
They take an octobus!

What's a sharks favourite game?
Bite and seek!

How do you make an octopus laugh?
With TEN-tickles!

Where does a mermaid keep her money?
In the riverbank!

Why don't mermaids play tennis?
Because they might get caught in the net!

Why do fish live in salt water?
Because pepper makes them sneeze!

What sits at the bottom of the ocean and trembles?
A nervous wreck!

Why don't oysters give to charity?
Because they're shellfish!

Which fish go to heaven when they die?
Angel fish!

What do you get from a bad-tempered shark?
As far away as possible!

How do all the oceans say hello to each other?
They wave!

What does a dolphin say when he's confused?
"Can you please be more Pacific!"

What did the shark say when he ate the clown fish?
"This tastes a little funny!"

Why did the crab get arrested?
Because he was always pinching things!

What do you call a fish that wears a bow tie?
Sofishticated!

How did the lobster get to the ocean?
By shell-icopter!

What do you get when you cross a snowman and a shark?
Frostbite!

Why is a fish easy to weigh?
Because he has his own scales!

What's the difference between a fish and a piano?
You can't tuna fish!

What did the sea say to the Little Mermaid?
Nothing, it just waved!

What do vampires cross the sea in?
Blood vessels!

Where do mummies go swimming?
The Dead Sea!

Which are the strongest creatures in the ocean?
Mussels!

Why are there fish at the bottom of the sea?
Because they dropped out of school!

What fish costs the most?
A gold fish!

What fish only swim at night
Starfish!

What kind of fish goes well with ice cream?
Jelly fish!

CHAPTER 8: DIZZY DINOSAURS!

WELCOME TO THE PREHISTORIC PLAYGROUND OF "DIZZY DINOSAURS" WHERE LAUGHTER ROARS LOUDER THAN A T-REX AND PUNS ARE AS OLD AS THE JURASSIC ERA!

GET READY TO TRAVEL BACK IN TIME AND UNLEASH YOUR INNER PALEONTOLOGIST WITH A COLLECTION OF RIB-TICKLING JOKES THAT WILL MAKE YOU DINO-MITE WITH LAUGHTER.

FROM PUNNY RAPTOR RIDDLES TO HILARIOUS T-REX ANTICS, THIS CHAPTER IS A FOSSILIZED TREASURE TROVE OF LAUGHTER THAT WILL HAVE YOU STOMPING YOUR FEET AND ROARING WITH DELIGHT.

SO GRAB YOUR ARCHAEOLOGIST HAT, DIG INTO THESE JOKES, AND GET READY TO HAVE A ROARING GOOD TIME THAT'S MILLIONS OF YEARS IN THE MAKING!

What does a triceratops sit on?
It's tricerabottom!

Why did dinosaurs eat raw meat?
Because they didn't know how to cook!

What do you call a tyrannosaurus that talks and talks and talks?
A dino-bore!

What game does the brontosaurus like to play?
Squash!

Why can't you hear a pterodactyl go to the toilet?
Because the pee is silent!

What do you call a dinosaur with an extensive vocabulary?
A thesaurus!

What do you get when a dinosaur walks through a strawberry patch?
Strawberry jam!

What do you call a dinosaur with one eye?
Do-you-think-he-saw-us!

Why did the dinosaur cross the road?
There weren't any chickens in those days!

What do you call a dinosaur in a phone booth?
Stuck!

Why don't you see dinosaurs at Easter?
Because they're eggs-tinct!

What makes more noise than a dinosaur?
Two dinosaurs!

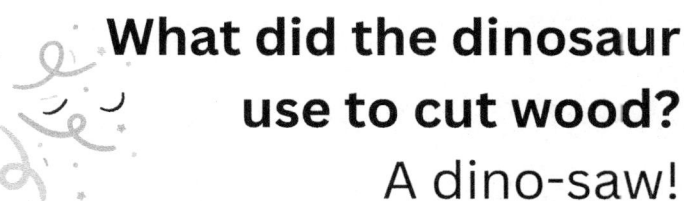

What did the dinosaur use to cut wood?
A dino-saw!

What do you call a dinosaur that doesn't take a bath?
Stink-o-Saurus!

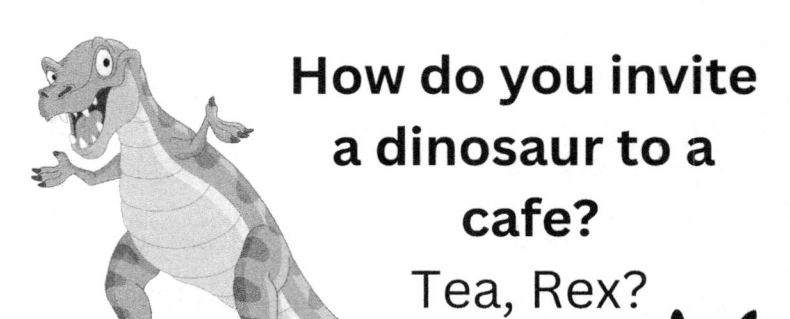

How do you invite a dinosaur to a cafe?
Tea, Rex?

93

What do you get when you cross a dinosaur with fireworks?
Dino-mite!

What do you get when a dinosaur sneezes?
Out of the way!

What do you call twin dinosaurs?
Pair-odactyls!

What do you get when a dinosaur crashes its car?
A Tyrannosaurus-WRECK!

What do you get when you cross a triceratops with a kangaroo?
A tricera-hops!

What do you call a dinosaur with a banana in each ear?
Anything you like, he can't hear you!

Why should you never ask a dinosaur to read you a story?
Because their tales are so long!

What do you call a dinosaur that's always late?
A Stegnosnorus!

What do you call a dinosaur that is sleeping?
A dino-snore!

What do you get when you cross a pig and a dinosaur?
Jurassic Pork!

What do you call a dinosaur that never gives up?
Try-try-try-ceratops!

CHAPTER 9: DAFT DOCTORS!

WELCOME TO THE HILARIOUS WORLD OF "DAFT DOCTORS" WHERE LAUGHTER IS THE BEST MEDICINE AND PUNCHLINES ARE DELIVERED WITH A DOSE OF GIGGLES!

GET READY FOR A COLLECTION OF HILARIOUS MEDICAL MISHAPS AND DOCTOR-RELATED HUMOUR.

FROM AMUSING ANECDOTES ABOUT FUNNY DIAGNOSES TO PLAYFUL INTERACTIONS BETWEEN PATIENTS AND DOCTORS, THIS CHAPTER IS A PRESCRIPTION FOR ENDLESS AMUSEMENT.

SO GET READY TO HEAL THOSE FUNNY BONES WITH THESE SIDE-SPLITTING JOKES THAT WILL LEAVE YOU IN STITCHES!

"Doctor, doctor, I think I'm turning into a pony!"
"Don't worry, it's not as bad as you think. You're just a little hoarse!"

"Doctor, doctor, I've got wind! Can you give me something!"
"Yes - here's a kite!"

"Doctor, doctor, I've got a pain in my lower back!"
"We must get to the bottom of this!"

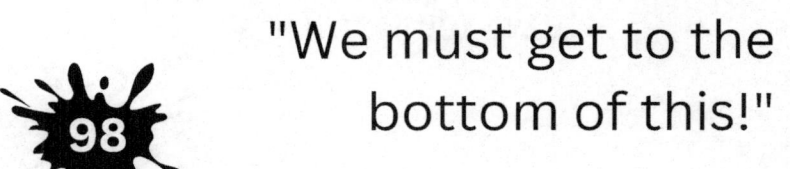

"Doctor, doctor, I keep thinking I'm a strawberry!"
"My, my, you're in a bit of a jam, then!"

"Doctor, doctor, I feel like a bucket!"
"You look a bit pale!"

"Doctor, doctor, people keep ignoring me!"
"Who said that?"

"Doctor, doctor, I feel like an apple!"
"We'll get to the core of this!"

"Doctor, doctor, everyone keeps throwing me in the garbage!"
"Don't talk rubbish!"

"Doctor, doctor, I feel like a pack of cards!"
"I'll deal with you later!"

"Doctor, doctor, I feel like a sheep!"
"Oh that's very baaaaaad!"

"Doctor, doctor, I think I'm a burglar!"
"Have you taken anything for it?"

"Doctor, doctor, how do I stop my nose from running?"
"Stick your foot out and trip it up!"

Why did the book go to the doctor?
He broke his spine!

"Doctor, doctor, I keep hearing a ringing sound!"
"Then answer the phone!"

"Doctor, doctor, I think I'm starting to look like a toilet!"
"Ah, yes, now you mention it, you do seem flushed!"

CHAPTER 10: COSMIC COMEDY!

3... 2... 1... BLAST OFF INTO THE INTERGALACTIC HILARITY OF "COSMIC COMEDY!"

GET READY FOR AN ASTRONOMICAL ADVENTURE AS WE EXPLORE THE COSMOS OF LAUGHTER AND JOURNEY THROUGH A GALAXY OF PUNS.

FROM OUT-OF-THIS-WORLD ONE-LINERS TO COMICAL ENCOUNTERS WITH ALIENS, THIS CHAPTER IS A STELLAR COLLECTION OF JOKES THAT WILL HAVE YOU LAUGHING LIKE SHOOTING STARS.

SO BUCKLE UP, PUT ON YOUR IMAGINARY SPACESUIT, AND PREPARE FOR A COSMIC JOURNEY FILLED WITH LAUGHTER, WHERE THE SKY IS NOT THE LIMIT, BUT THE LAUNCHPAD FOR ASTRONOMICAL AMUSEMENT!

How do you stop an astronaut's baby from crying?
You rocket!

How does NASA organise a party?
They planet!

What is an astronaut's favorite chocolate?
A Mars bar!

I'm reading a book about anti-gravity...
It's impossible to put down!

What do you call a spaceship that drips water?
A crying saucer!

Why is Buzz Lightyear so good at maths?
Because he can count to infinity and beyond!

What dance do all astronauts know?
The moonwalk!

What was the first animal in space?
The cow that jumped over the moon!

What do you think of that new cafe on the moon?
Food was great, but there really wasn't must atmosphere!

What do planets like to read?
Comet books!

What do you call a peanut in a spacesuit?
An astro-nut!

Why don't aliens eat clowns?
Because they taste funny!

What do you call a pan spinning through space?
An unidentified frying object!

Why did the sun go to school?
To get brighter!

What do martians serve their dinner on?
Flying saucers!

How do aliens keep their pants up?
With an asteroid belt!

How do you know when the moon has enough to eat?
When it's full!

How does the man in the moon eat his food?
In satellite dishes!

Why did the cow go to outer space?
To visit the milky way!

Why didn't the sun go to college?
It already had a million degrees!

What's an astronauts favourite key on the keyboard?
The space bar!

Why did Micky Mouse go to outer space?
He was looking for Pluto!

Why can't aliens play golf in space?
Too many black holes!

How do aliens pay for coffee?
With starbucks!

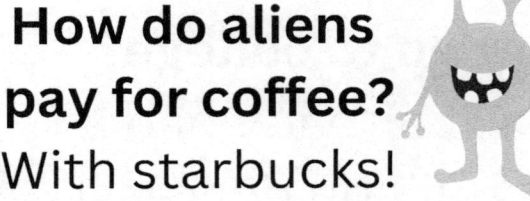

Why couldn't the astronaut book a room on the moon?
It was full!

What did Mars say to Saturn?
"Give me a ring sometime!"

What is an astronauts favourite snack?
Space chips!

Why did the alien go to the doctor?
He looked a little green!

Astronomers got bored of watching the world spin.
So they decided to call it a day!

CHAPTER 11: DOOR KNOCKERS!

OPEN THE DOOR TO ENDLESS LAUGHTER WITH "DOOR KNOCKERS" OUR COLLECTION OF KNOCK KNOCK JOKES, WHERE HILARITY AWAITS ON THE OTHER SIDE!

GET READY TO ENGAGE IN A DELIGHTFUL GAME OF COMEDIC DOORBELL RINGING AS WE EXPLORE A COLLECTION OF RIB-TICKLING KNOCK KNOCK JOKES.

FROM SILLY WORDPLAY TO UNEXPECTED PUNCHLINES, THIS CHAPTER IS A GATEWAY TO LAUGHTER THAT WILL HAVE YOU EAGERLY ANTICIPATING EACH "WHO'S THERE?" MOMENT.

"Knock, knock!"
"Who's there?"
"Wooden"
"Wooden who?"
"Wooden you like to know!"

"Knock, knock"
"Who's there?"
"Spell"
"Spell who?"
"W. H. O!"

"Knock, knock!"
"Who's there?"
"Atch"
"Atch who?"
"Bless you!"

"Knock, knock!"
"Who's there?"
"Cash"
"Cash who?"
"I knew you were a nut!"

"Knock, knock"
"Who's there?"
"Kanga"
"Kanga who?"
"Actually it's kangaroo!"

"Knock, knock!"
"Who's there?"
"Doctor"
"Doctor who?"
"You just said it!"

"Knock, knock!"
"Who's there?"
"Cows go"
"Cows go who?"
"No silly, cows go MOO!"

"Knock, knock"
"Who's there?"
"A little old lady"
"A little old lady who?"
"I didn't know you could yodel!"

"Knock, knock!"
"Who's there?"
"Tank"
"Tank who?"
"You're welcome!"

"Knock, knock!"
"Who's there?"
"Woo"
"Woo who?"
"Why are you so excited?"

"Knock, knock"
"Who's there?"
"The interrupting cow"
"The interrupting co-MOOOOOOO!"

"Knock, knock!"
"Who's there?"
"Boo"
"Boo who?"
"Don't cry, it's just a joke!"

"Knock, knock!"
"Who's there?"
"Lettuce"
"Lettuce who?"
"Lettuce in, it's cold out here!"

"Knock, knock"
"Who's there?"
"Goat"
"Goat who?"
"Goat to the door and find out!"

"Knock, knock!"
"Who's there?"
"Annie"
"Annie who?"
"Annie body home?"

"Knock, knock!"
"Who's there?"
"Radio"
"Radio who?"
"Radio not, here I come"

"Knock, knock"
"Who's there?"
"Witches"
"Witches who"
"Witches the best way out of this neighborhood?"

"Knock, knock!"
"Who's there?"
"Done a"
"Done a who?"
"You did a poo!"

"Knock, knock!"
"Who's there?"
"Noah"
"Noah who?"
"Know a place I can spend the night?"

"Knock, knock"
"Who's there?"
"Queen"
"Queen who?"
"Queen your room. It's filthy"

"Knock, knock!"
"Who's there?"
"Luke"
"Luke who?"
"Luke through the peep hole and find out!"

CHAPTER 12: SPOOKY SNIGGERS!

PREPARE FOR A SPINE-TINGLING ADVENTURE WITH "SPOOKY SNIGGERS" WHERE LAUGHTER MEETS THE SUPERNATURAL IN A HAUNTINGLY HILARIOUS WAY!

STEP INTO THE SHADOWS AS WE UNLEASH A COLLECTION OF GHOULISHLY FUNNY JOKES THAT WILL MAKE YOU SCREAM... WITH LAUGHTER!

FROM HILARIOUS GHOSTLY ENCOUNTERS TO WICKEDLY WITTY WITCHCRAFT, THIS CHAPTER IS A CAULDRON FULL OF GIGGLES AND GAGS THAT WILL SEND SHIVERS OF AMUSEMENT DOWN YOUR SPINE.

SO GATHER ROUND, BRAVE SOULS, AND GET READY TO BE SPOOKED IN THIS SPOOKTACULAR CHAPTER THAT WILL HAVE YOU HOWLING WITH LAUGHTER ALL THROUGH THE NIGHT!

How do you get a witch to itch?
You take away the 'w'!

How do ghosts like their eggs?
Terror-fried!

How does a ghost sneeze?
Ahh...ahh...ahh...BOO!

What day do ghosts do their howling?
On Moan-day!

What do ghosts eat for dinner?
Spook-etti!

What did the skeleton order at the restaurant?
Spare ribs!

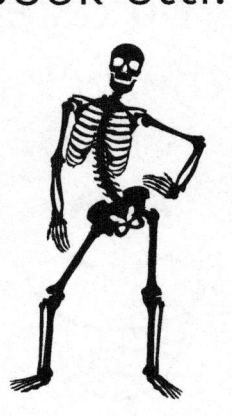

Who was the most famous skeleton detective?
Sherlock Bones!

Why do witches wear name tags?
So they know which witch is which!

Why do undertakers often catch colds?
Because they're always surrounded by coffin!

Why did the skeleton go to the party alone?
Because he had no body to dance with!

Why did Frankenstein go to the evening classes?
Because they had a body-building session!

Why did the zombie take a sick day?
He was feeling really rotten!

Are there any Halloween monsters good at math?
No - unless you Count Dracula!

Why don't skeletons fight each other?
They don't have the guts!

Do undertakers enjoy their job?
Of corpse the do!

What did the monster eat after having all his teeth taken out?
The dentist!

Why are mummies good at keeping secrets?
Because they keep things under wraps!

What's a vampire's favourite fruit?
A blood orange!

What does a vampire doctor say?
Necks, please!

Why didn't the skeleton go to school?
His heart wasn't in it!

What kind of spirits haunt hospitals?
Surgical spirits!

What room does a ghost not need?
A living room!

What do birds say on Halloween?
Trick or Tweet!

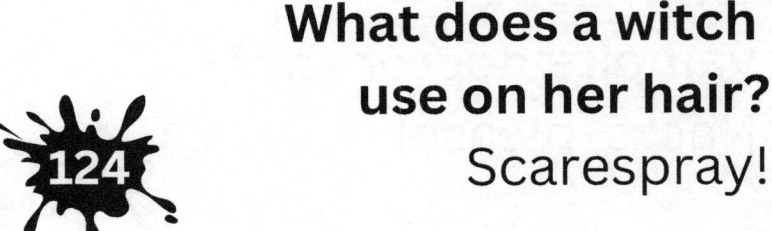

What does a witch use on her hair?
Scarespray!

Why is there always a fence around a graveyard?
Because people are dying to get in!

Why couldn't Dracula's wife get to sleep?
Because she was kept awake by her husband's coffin!

Why was there thunder and lightning in the lab?
Because the scientists were brainstorming!

Why did the skeleton go to the barbecue?
He needed some spare ribs!

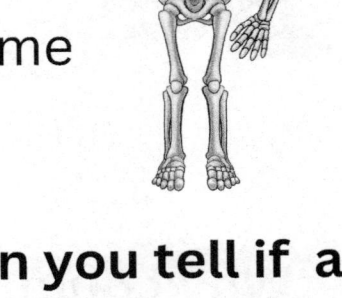

How can you tell if a vampire has a cold?
They start coffin!

Why are ghosts bad liars?
Because you can see right through them!

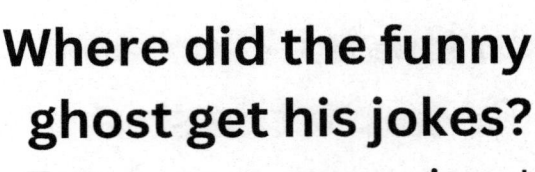

Where did the funny ghost get his jokes?
From a crypt writer!

What does a ghost keep in his cellar?
Whines and spirits!

How does a ghost pass through a locked door?
It uses a skeleton key!

What is a witch's favourite class?
Spelling!

What type of plates do skeletons like to use?
Bone china!

Where do ghosts like to travel on vacation?
The Dead Sea!

What's a ghost's favourite dessert?
I scream!

Why did the skeleton laugh?
Because it had a funny bone!

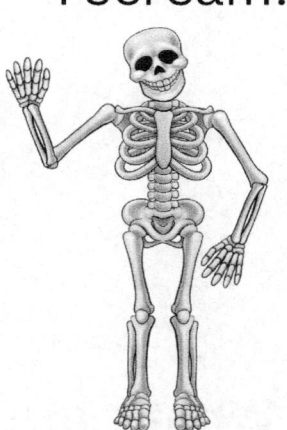

What's a skeleton's favourite instrument?
A sax-a-bone!

What's a zombie's favourite cereal?
Rice Creepies!

What's it like being kissed by a vampire?
It's a pain in the neck!

What did one ghost say to the other?
Get a life!

Where do fashionable ghosts shop?
Bootiques!

Why can't a vampire go to a barbecue?
They're afraid of stakes.

Why did the skeleton climb up the tree?
Because a dog was after his bones!

Wanna know why skeletons are so calm?
Because nothing gets under their skin!

What do you call a skeleton who won't get up in the mornings?
Lazy bones!

Do zombies eat burgers with their fingers?
No, they eat the fingers separately!

What monster plays tricks on Halloween?
Prank-enstein!

What does a headless horseman ride?
A nightmare!

What do you call two witches living together?
Broomates!

What's big, scary and has three wheels?
A monster on a tricycle!

What happens when a witch loses her temper?
She flies off the handle!

What entertainment do ghosts attend at Christmas?
Phantomimes!

Where do ghosts like to trick or treat?
Dead ends!

What do short-sighted ghosts wear?
Spooktacles!

CHAPTER 13: FUNNY FOOD

WELCOME TO THE DELICIOUSLY DAFT WORLD OF "FUNNY FOOD" WHERE LAUGHTER IS THE SECRET INGREDIENT THAT MAKES EVERY MEAL TASTE BETTER!

GET READY TO FEAST ON A BUFFET OF BELLY LAUGHS AS WE SERVE UP A DELECTABLE COLLECTION OF FOOD-THEMED JOKES AND PUNS.

FROM CHEESY ONE-LINERS TO SAUCY PUNCHLINES, THIS CHAPTER WILL SATISFY YOUR CRAVINGS FOR LAUGHTER.

SO PREPARE YOUR TASTE BUDS FOR A HILARIOUS TREAT, AND GET READY TO DEVOUR THESE FOOD-INSPIRED JOKES THAT WILL LEAVE YOU HUNGRY FOR MORE!

What's the rudest vegetable?
Pea!

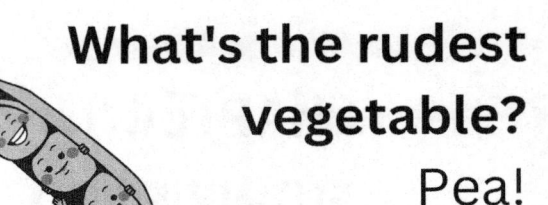

What kind of keys do kids like to carry?
Cookies!

Where do cucumbers go for a drink?
The salad bar!

What's a deer's favourite ice cream flavour?
Cookie doe!

What did the real noodle call the fake noodle?
An impasta!

What did the grape say when it got stepped on?
Nothing, it just let out a little whine!

Why can't an egg tell a joke?
Because it will crack up!

What did the french fry say to the slow hamburger?
Ketchup!

Why did the banana go to the doctors?
Because it wasn't peeling well!

What did the mayonnaise say to the fridge?
Close the door, I'm dressing!

Do you want to hear a joke about the pizza?
Never mind, it's too cheesy!

What sound does a nut make when it sneezes?
Ca-shew!

Why did the orange lose the race?
It ran out of juice!

What's the difference between roast beef and pea soup?
Anyone can roast beef!

What's a vegetable's favourite kind of joke?
A corny joke!

What did the macaroni say to the tomato?
"Don't get saucy with me!"

Why did the pod excuse itself from the dinner table?
It had to pea!

What kind of bean doesn't grow in your garden?
A jelly bean!

What did the little corn say to the mama corn?
"Where is pop corn?"

What did one plate say to the other plate?
"Dinner is on me!"

Where do hamburgers go to dance?
They go to the meatball!

Why did the mushroom go to the party?
Because he was a fungi to be with!

What's yellow and extremely stupid?
Thick custard!

Why did the cookie go to the doctor?
Because it felt crummy!

Why did the tomato turn red?
Because it saw the salad dressing!

Why was the fruit busy on Friday night?
It had a date!

How can you get breakfast in bed?
Sleep in the kitchen!

What's a banana's favourite way to say "thank you?"
Thanks a bunch!

What did the strawberry write to its crush?
I'm berry fond of you!

Where do you learn to make banana splits?
At sundae school!

Why was the baby strawberry crying?
Because her mom and dad were in a jam!

Why doesn't the corn like the farmer?
Because he picks his ears!

What's worse than finding a worm in your apple?
Finding half a worm!

Why did the grape stop in the middle of the road?
It ran out of juice!

What do you give a sick lemon?
Lemon-aid!

What do you call a sad strawberry?
A blueberry!

Why did the vegetable call the plumber?
It had a leek!

What's the best day to eat toffees?
Chews-day!

CHAPTER 14: WAITER WISECRACKS!

STEP INTO THE WACKY WORLD OF THE "WAITER WISECRACKS" WHERE LAUGHTER IS ALWAYS ON THE MENU AND THE PUNCHLINES ARE SERVED WITH A SIDE OF SILLINESS!

GET READY TO DINE ON A PLATTER OF HILARIOUS WAITER ANTICS AND COMICAL RESTAURANT HUMOR.

FROM MIX-UPS WITH ORDERS TO FUNNY ENCOUNTERS WITH CLUMSY SERVERS, THIS CHAPTER IS A FEAST OF LAUGHTER THAT WILL HAVE YOU TIPPING OVER WITH AMUSEMENT.

SO, SIT BACK, AND GET READY TO BE SERVED A HEAPING PORTION OF SIDE-SPLITTING JOKES THAT WILL LEAVE YOU LAUGHING TILL DESSERT!

"Waiter, waiter, this soup tastes funny!"
"Then why aren't you laughing?"

"Waiter, waiter, what's this fly doing in my soup?"
"It looks like it's learning to swim!"

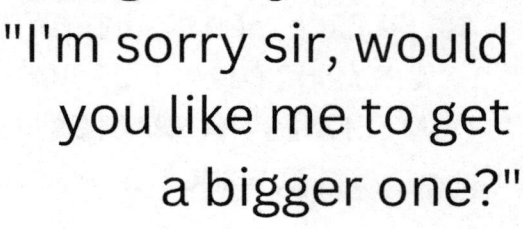

"Waiter, waiter, there is a small slug in my lettuce"
"I'm sorry sir, would you like me to get a bigger one?"

"Waiter, waiter, there's a fly in my soup!"
"Don't worry sir, that spider on your bread will soon get him!"

"Waiter, waiter, bring me something to eat and make it snappy!"
"How about a crocodile sandwich, sir?"

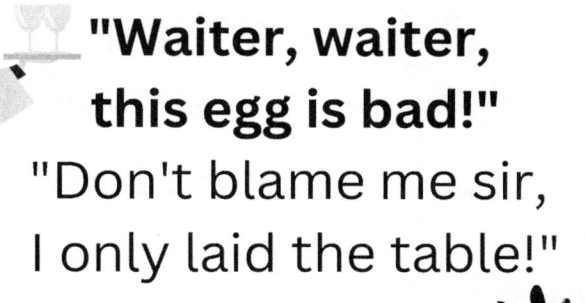

"Waiter, waiter, this egg is bad!"
"Don't blame me sir, I only laid the table!"

"Waiter, waiter, what's this spider doing in my alphabet soup?"
"Probably trying to read, sir!"

"Waiter, waiter, there's a button in my stew!"
"It expect it fell off the jacket potato, sir!"

"Waiter, waiter, do you have chicken legs?"
"No sir, I always walk like this!"

CHAPTER 15: CHRISTMAS CRACKERS!

STEP INTO A WINTER WONDERLAND OF LAUGHTER WITH "CHRISTMAS CRACKERS" WHERE HOLIDAY HILARITY AND FESTIVE FUN TAKE CENTER STAGE!

GET READY TO JINGLE ALL THE WAY WITH A COLLECTION OF RIB-TICKLING JOKES THAT WILL MAKE YOUR HOLIDAY SEASON MERRIER THAN EVER.

FROM SANTA'S BELLY-SHAKING LAUGHS TO SNOWMAN SHENANIGANS, THIS CHAPTER IS A GIFT-WRAPPED PACKAGE OF LAUGHTER THAT WILL HAVE YOU HO-HO-HO-ING WITH DELIGHT.

SO GRAB A CUP OF COCOA, COZY UP BY THE FIREPLACE, AND GET READY TO BE FILLED WITH THE SPIRIT OF JOY AND LAUGHTER AS YOU UNWRAP THESE SIDE-SPLITTING JOKES THAT WILL LEAVE YOU IN FITS OF CHRISTMAS MIRTH!

What did Santa's dog ask for this Christmas?
A mobile bone!

Which of Santa's reindeer has the best moves?
Dancer!

What do Santa's elves do after school?
Their gnome work!

Who is Santa's favourite singer?
Beyon-sleigh!

Why did the elf go to school?
To learn his elf-abet!

Why did the Christmas turkey form a band?
It had the drumsticks!

What is a parent's favourite Christmas carol?
Silent Night!

Who hides in the bakery at Christmas?
A mince spy!

What did Santa say on Christmas morning?
That's a wrap!

Why did Santa get a ticket on Christmas Eve?
Because he parked his sleigh in the snow parking zone!

What do you get when you cross a snowman and a baker?
Frosty the Dough-man!

Why did Rudolph the red-nosed reindeer have a bad report card?
Because he went down in history!

Why are Christmas trees like bad knitters?
They both drop needles!

Why does Santa have a garden?
So he can hoe, hoe, hoe!

Why is a foot a good Christmas gift?
It fits the right stocking!

Why does Santa Claus like to go down the chimney?
Because it soots him!

What do you get when you cross a snowman and a vampire?
Frostbite!

What happened to the man who stole a calendar at Christmas?
He got 12 months!

Why did Santa get stuck in the chimney?
Because he ate too many cookies!

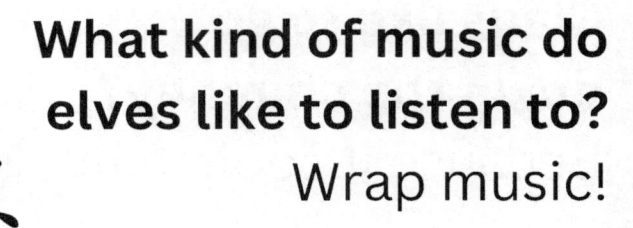

What kind of music do elves like to listen to?
Wrap music!

What did Santa say at the start of the race?
"Ready, set, ho, ho, ho!"

Why doesn't Santa go to hospital?
He doesn't have elf care!

Why is one of Santa's reindeer's always in trouble?
Because he was RUDE-olph!

Why are Christmas trees so bad at sewing?
They always drop their needles!

153

What's the most popular Christmas wine?
"I don't like Brussel sprouts!"

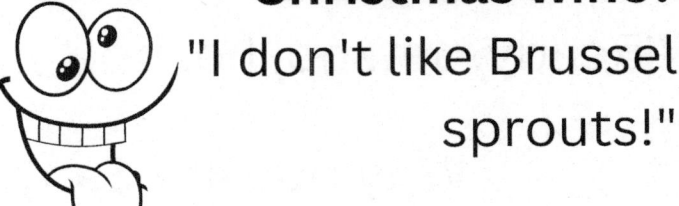

What do you call Santa when he takes a break?
Santa pause!

Why do mummies like Christmas so much?
Because of all the wrapping!

What do monkeys sing at Christmas?
Jungle bells, jungle bells!

Printed in Great Britain
by Amazon